Christmas 2020

Dear Everett,

    We hope you enjoy reading this devotional to Dad and Mom and Baby Sister!

    We pray the Lord will hold you close and keep you in His care.

All our love,
Grampy and
Grammy

PRESENTED TO

_____

FROM

_____

ON THIS DATE

_____

"Remember, LORD, how I have walked before you
faithfully and with wholehearted devotion and
have done what is good in your eyes."

ISAIAH 38:3 NIV

# Night Night
## Devotions

90
DEVOTIONS
FOR
BEDTIME

AMY PARKER

illustrated by
VIRGINIA ALLYN

An Imprint of Thomas Nelson
thomasnelson.com

*Night Night Devotions*

© 2019 by Amy Parker

Published in Nashville, Tennessee, by Tommy Nelson. Tommy Nelson is an imprint of Thomas Nelson. Thomas Nelson is a registered trademark of HarperCollins Christian Publishing, Inc.

Illustrated by Virginia Allyn

Tommy Nelson titles may be purchased in bulk for educational, business, fund-raising, or sales promotional use. For information, please email SpecialMarkets@ThomasNelson.com.

Unless otherwise noted, Scripture is quoted from the International Children's Bible®, copyright ©1986, 1988, 1999, 2015 by Tommy Nelson®. Used by permission.

Scripture noted "NASB" is taken from the NEW AMERICAN STANDARD BIBLE®, Copyright © 1960, 1962, 1963, 1968, 1971, 1972, 1973, 1975, 1977, 1995 by The Lockman Foundation. Used by permission.

Scripture noted "NCV" is from the New Century Version®. Copyright © 2005 by Thomas Nelson. Used by permission. All rights reserved.

Scripture noted "NIV" is from THE HOLY BIBLE, NEW INTERNATIONAL VERSION®, NIV® Copyright © 1973, 1978, 1984, 2011 by Biblica, Inc.® Used by permission. All rights reserved worldwide.

Scripture noted "NKJV" is taken from the New King James Version®. Copyright © 1982 by Thomas Nelson. Used by permission. All rights reserved.

**Library of Congress Cataloging-in-Publication Data is on file.**

ISBN-13: 978-1-4002-0890-6

*Printed in China*

19 20 21 22 23 DSC 6 5 4 3 2 1

Mfr: DSC / Shenzhen, China / October 2019 / PO # 9549947

To Mr. & Mrs. Parker,
for more than fifty years of devotion
to your family and each other

# Contents

*A Letter to Parents* . . . . . . . . . . . . . . . . . . . . . . . 15

## DEVOTIONS FROM THE OLD TESTAMENT

When the World Was Made . . . . . . . . . . . . . . . . . . . 18
*Genesis 1:1*

It Is Very Good . . . . . . . . . . . . . . . . . . . . . . 20
*Genesis 1:31*

The Big No-No . . . . . . . . . . . . . . . . . . . 22
*Genesis 3:12*

Noah Obeys (No Matter What) . . . . . . . . . . . . 24
*Genesis 6:9*

Abraham's Promise . . . . . . . . . . . . . . . . 26
*Genesis 15:6*

Your Shield, Your Reward . . . . . . . . . . . . . . 28
*Genesis 15:1*

Is Anything Too Hard? . . . . . . . . . . . . . . . 30
*Genesis 18:14*

God Is There . . . . . . . . . . . . . . . . . . . 32
*Genesis 28:15*

Joseph, the Dreamer . . . . . . . . . . . . . . . . 34
*Genesis 37:19*

Turning into Good . . . . . . . . . . . . . . . . . . . . . 36
   *Genesis 50:20*
Splitting the Sea . . . . . . . . . . . . . . . . . . . . . 38
   *Exodus 14:14*
What If? . . . . . . . . . . . . . . . . . . . . . . . . . . 40
   *Exodus 3:12*
Who Is Like You? . . . . . . . . . . . . . . . . . . . . 42
   *Exodus 15:11*
Your Promise . . . . . . . . . . . . . . . . . . . . . . . 44
   *Exodus 15:13*
Honor Your Parents . . . . . . . . . . . . . . . . . . 46
   *Exodus 20:12*
Time for Rest . . . . . . . . . . . . . . . . . . . . . . . 48
   *Exodus 20:10*
Love Your Neighbor . . . . . . . . . . . . . . . . . . 50
   *Leviticus 19:18*
God of Mercy . . . . . . . . . . . . . . . . . . . . . . . 52
   *Deuteronomy 4:31*
With Everything . . . . . . . . . . . . . . . . . . . . . 54
   *Deuteronomy 6:5*
A Donkey Talks . . . . . . . . . . . . . . . . . . . . . 56
   *Numbers 22:32*
Strong and Brave . . . . . . . . . . . . . . . . . . . . 58
   *Joshua 1:9*
Joshua and the Big Wall . . . . . . . . . . . . . . . 60
   *Joshua 6:5*

Serve the Lord . . . . . . . . . . . . . . . . . . . . . 62
  *Joshua 24:15*
The Wimpy Warrior . . . . . . . . . . . . . . . . . . 64
  *Judges 6:12*
God Calls Samuel . . . . . . . . . . . . . . . . . . . 66
  *1 Samuel 3:10*
The Great Big Meanie . . . . . . . . . . . . . . . . 68
  *1 Samuel 17:45*
The World's Wisest King . . . . . . . . . . . . . . 70
  *1 Kings 3:9*
The World's Bravest Queen . . . . . . . . . . . . 72
  *Esther 4:14*
You Keep Me Safe . . . . . . . . . . . . . . . . . . . 74
  *Psalm 4:8*
When Trouble Comes . . . . . . . . . . . . . . . . 76
  *Psalm 46:1*
Rejoice and Be Glad! . . . . . . . . . . . . . . . . 78
  *Psalm 118:24*
God Never Sleeps . . . . . . . . . . . . . . . . . . . 80
  *Psalm 121:3*
Amazing Me! . . . . . . . . . . . . . . . . . . . . . . . 82
  *Psalm 139:14*
Heart Healer . . . . . . . . . . . . . . . . . . . . . . . 84
  *Psalm 147:3*
Star Counter . . . . . . . . . . . . . . . . . . . . . . . 86
  *Psalm 147:4*

Trust the Lord. . . . . . . . . . . . . . . . . . . . . . . . 88
  *Proverbs 3:5*

Love Forgives All. . . . . . . . . . . . . . . . . . . . . . 90
  *Proverbs 10:12*

Prince of Peace. . . . . . . . . . . . . . . . . . . . . . . 92
  *Isaiah 9:6*

Strong Again . . . . . . . . . . . . . . . . . . . . . . . . 94
  *Isaiah 40:31*

Your God . . . . . . . . . . . . . . . . . . . . . . . . . . 96
  *Isaiah 41:10*

Good Plans . . . . . . . . . . . . . . . . . . . . . . . . . 98
  *Jeremiah 29:11*

A Brand-New Day . . . . . . . . . . . . . . . . . . . . . 100
  *Lamentations 3:22–23*

Daniel Is Safe. . . . . . . . . . . . . . . . . . . . . . . 102
  *Daniel 6:27*

Jonah Doesn't Obey (at First) . . . . . . . . . . . . . . 104
  *Jonah 2:7*

Rest in His Love . . . . . . . . . . . . . . . . . . . . . . 106
  *Zephaniah 3:17*

## DEVOTIONS FROM THE NEW TESTAMENT

An Angel Visits Mary and Joseph . . . . . . . . . . . . . 110
  *Luke 1:37*

A Miracle in a Stable . . . . . . . . . . . . . . . . . . . . 112
   *Luke 2:11*
Angels in the Sky. . . . . . . . . . . . . . . . . . . . . . 114
   *Luke 2:20*
Jesus in His Father's House . . . . . . . . . . . . . . . . 116
   *Luke 2:49*
Follow, Follow Me! . . . . . . . . . . . . . . . . . . . . . 118
   *Mark 1:17*
Make Peace . . . . . . . . . . . . . . . . . . . . . . . . . 120
   *Matthew 5:9*
Jesus Calms a Storm. . . . . . . . . . . . . . . . . . . . 122
   *Mark 4:39*
God Loves You *So* Much. . . . . . . . . . . . . . . . . . 124
   *John 3:16*
Whoever Believes . . . . . . . . . . . . . . . . . . . . . 126
   *John 3:16*
A Boy Shares His Lunch . . . . . . . . . . . . . . . . . . 128
   *John 6:9*
Jesus Walks on Water . . . . . . . . . . . . . . . . . . . 130
   *Matthew 14:29*
Jesus Heals . . . . . . . . . . . . . . . . . . . . . . . . . 132
   *Matthew 9:25*
Jesus Loves You . . . . . . . . . . . . . . . . . . . . . . 134
   *Matthew 19:14*
Light of the World . . . . . . . . . . . . . . . . . . . . . 136
   *John 8:12*

The Nice Neighbor . . . . . . . . . . . . . . . . . . . . . . 138
   *Luke 10:37*
"If You Can" . . . . . . . . . . . . . . . . . . . . . . . . 140
   *Mark 9:23*
Jesus Washes Feet . . . . . . . . . . . . . . . . . . . . 142
   *John 13:14*
Jesus Lives . . . . . . . . . . . . . . . . . . . . . . . . 144
   *Matthew 28:6*
Go Tell the World! . . . . . . . . . . . . . . . . . . . 146
   *Matthew 28:19*
Not Like the World . . . . . . . . . . . . . . . . . . . 148
   *John 14:27*
Love Like Jesus . . . . . . . . . . . . . . . . . . . . . 150
   *John 15:12*
Be Brave! . . . . . . . . . . . . . . . . . . . . . . . . . 152
   *John 16:33*
Believe in the Lord . . . . . . . . . . . . . . . . . . . 154
   *Acts 16:31*
For the Good . . . . . . . . . . . . . . . . . . . . . . . 156
   *Romans 8:28*
Pray Always . . . . . . . . . . . . . . . . . . . . . . . . 158
   *Romans 12:12*
Love Is . . . . . . . . . . . . . . . . . . . . . . . . . . . 160
   *1 Corinthians 13:4*
Faith, Hope, and Love . . . . . . . . . . . . . . . . . 162
   *1 Corinthians 13:13*

So Many Blessings . . . . . . . . . . . . . . . . . . . . . 164
  *2 Corinthians 9:8*
When You Are Weak. . . . . . . . . . . . . . . . . . . . 166
  *2 Corinthians 12:9*
The Best Fruit. . . . . . . . . . . . . . . . . . . . . . . 168
  *Galatians 5:22–23*
That Love . . . . . . . . . . . . . . . . . . . . . . . . . 170
  *Ephesians 3:18*
Ask God . . . . . . . . . . . . . . . . . . . . . . . . . . 172
  *Philippians 4:6*
God's Peace. . . . . . . . . . . . . . . . . . . . . . . . 174
  *Philippians 4:7*
Think Good Thoughts . . . . . . . . . . . . . . . . . . 176
  *Philippians 4:8*
I Can!. . . . . . . . . . . . . . . . . . . . . . . . . . . . 178
  *Philippians 4:13*
Always Give Thanks . . . . . . . . . . . . . . . . . . . 180
  *Colossians 3:15*
You Are Important! . . . . . . . . . . . . . . . . . . . 182
  *1 Timothy 4:12*
Be an Example . . . . . . . . . . . . . . . . . . . . . . 184
  *1 Timothy 4:12*
Your Superpowers . . . . . . . . . . . . . . . . . . . . 186
  *2 Timothy 1:7*
It's Alive!. . . . . . . . . . . . . . . . . . . . . . . . . . 188
  *Hebrews 4:12*

The Lord Cares for You . . . . . . . . . . . . . . . . . . . . . 190
*1 Peter 5:7*

You Are God's Child . . . . . . . . . . . . . . . . . . . . . . 192
*1 John 3:1*

Go Away, Fear! . . . . . . . . . . . . . . . . . . . . . . . . 194
*1 John 4:18*

The One Who Loves Us . . . . . . . . . . . . . . . . . . . 196
*Revelation 1:5*

Pictures of Heaven . . . . . . . . . . . . . . . . . . . . . . 198
*Revelation 1:8*

*About the Author* . . . . . . . . . . . . . . . . . . . . . . 201

# A Letter to Parents

**My dear readers,**

I'm so happy that you're simply holding this book. It means that you care about sharing the love of God. Sharing that love is, in my opinion, our most important job on this planet.

That's the essence of a devotional, isn't it? The word *devotion* means love, faithfulness, closeness, loyalty. Of course, our children need to know the story of God and His people, as shared in *Night Night Bible Stories*. But the sole purpose of this devotional is instilling that feeling of faithfulness and a lifetime of love for the God who loves them so much that He gave His only Son to save them.

So that you may use this as a companion to *Night Night Bible Stories*, I've written devotions with corresponding titles to accompany each Bible story, with lots more in between! No matter how you read them, it is my hope that these devotionals will reveal the never-ending love of God to your little ones—and to you.

I will be praying for you, dear readers, as you do this lovely work that He has called us to do.

**Night night,**

*Amy*
♡

# Devotions from the Old Testament

# When the World Was Made

In the beginning God created
the heavens and the earth.

—GENESIS 1:1 NIV

Close your eyes. Now think really hard about
something you want. Okay, now make it appear by
just saying it out loud.

Did it work? No? Do you know why? You're not God.

But that's what God did when He created the world.
All He had to do was say what He wanted: all the stars,
the planets, the trees, the flowers, the animals, and even
you and me.

He thought about a big, round moon and sparkly stars. He thought about Earth and Venus and Mercury and Mars. He thought about the stripes on the zebra and the buzz of the bee. He thought about a teeny, tiny clover and a big oak tree.

And do you know the best part? He thought about two eyes, two ears, and a little freckled nose. He thought about ten long fingers and ten short toes. Made in His image, soaked in His grace, God created the whole human race.

You and me—every last one of us. Everything on this planet and beyond. He dreamed it up and created it, just by saying the word. Amazing, huh?

And that's only the beginning.

Thank You, God, for the moon and stars,
For trees and bees, Mercury and Mars.
For zebra stripes and big oak trees.
Thank You, God, for creating me.

## Night night, God.

Right now, close your eyes and imagine the whole world taking shape. Amazing!

# It Is Very Good

God looked at everything he had
made, and it was very good.

—GENESIS 1:31

Do you ever look outside and think about how
beautiful the world is?
Sun streaming through wind-blown trees . . .
Birds singing and splashing in the fresh-fallen rain . . .
The smell of honeysuckles on a hot summer day . . .
The *crunch, crunch, crunch* of golden leaves . . .
Deer tiptoeing through the bright white snow . . .

Don't you smile just thinking about it all?

Sometimes, though, we get busy. Sometimes we focus on bad things in this world. Sometimes we think too much about what we *don't* have. And we forget about everything God created for us, all of the gifts waiting there in our homes and right outside our door, all of the beauty of this world.

When that happens, look out the window. Take a walk. Smell the flowers, and listen to the birds in your own backyard. Smile a big smile at that adorable face in the mirror. And thank God for everything that He gave us.

The beautiful world that God created—it's still out there. And it is *still* very good.

Help me to remember, God,
All that You've made for me.
Help me to look for good until
Your beauty is all that I see.

## Night night, God.

What is your favorite
thing that God created?

# The Big No-No

The man said, "You gave this
woman to me. She gave me fruit
from the tree. So I ate it."

—GENESIS 3:12

When you get caught in a big no-no, what do you do? Do you hide? Do you blame it on someone else? Or do you immediately admit it and say, "I'm sorry"?

In the first big no-no of the Bible, Adam and Eve did two of those things. First they hid, and then they blamed it on someone else. When God asked Adam what happened, Adam blamed it on Eve. "She gave me fruit from the tree." It even sounds like Adam blamed it on God when he pointed out that God "gave this woman" to him.

Then when God

asked Eve about it, she said, "The snake tricked me" (Genesis 3:13).

It's kind of silly when you think about it. The only person who made Adam's decision was Adam. And the only person who made Eve's decision was Eve.

When we do something wrong, it's usually tough to admit it. It's a lot easier to blame it on someone else, to say it was someone else's fault. But I bet you already know the right thing to do.

When you do something wrong, admit it. Say, "I'm sorry." And then try never to do that thing again. The best part is: no matter what you do, when you ask God to forgive you, His answer is always yes.

Thank You, God, for forgiving me
When I do something wrong;
Help me to be kind and good,
To always get along.

## Night night, God.

Do you need to ask for forgiveness for something? Talk to God about it right now.

# Noah Obeys (No Matter What)

Noah was a good man. . . .
He walked with God.

—GENESIS 6:9

It's hard to do the right thing sometimes. It's hard to choose the right thing when no one seems to notice. It's hard to do the right thing when everyone around you is doing the wrong thing. And it's *really* hard to do the right thing when the people doing wrong seem to be having a lot more fun!

Noah lived in a time when everyone around him was doing bad things. But Noah didn't choose what was easy. He didn't choose what seemed fun at the time.

He chose what was good. He chose walking with God. And God noticed.

Because Noah did the right thing, his entire family was saved in the big flood. And now even thousands of years after Noah walked the earth, we're still talking about Noah. When you read in the Bible about Noah, it says, "Noah was a good man. . . . He walked with God." What a wonderful way to be remembered!

Choose good. Choose godly. Even when it's hard. Even when no one seems to notice. Because God sees. He sees your hard choices, and He knows who walks with Him.

Dear God, lead me, please,
Help me to obey,
Help me to choose what is good,
Help me to walk in Your way.

## Night night, God.

In a hundred years, what will people be reading about you?

# Abraham's Promise

Abram believed the Lord.

—Genesis 15:6

God made Abraham (also called Abram) an amazing promise. He told Abraham that in the years to come the number of people in his family would be more than all the stars in the sky. That seems pretty impossible by itself. But then when you think that Abraham and Sarah were very old and *still* had no children, well, that promise seems unbelievable.

But Genesis 15:6 tells us that Abraham *believed* God. Even when it seemed unbelievable. Even when Abraham saw no possible way that it could happen. Even when he couldn't count all the stars in the sky. Abraham believed.

What about you? Do you believe God? Do you believe that He hears your prayers? Do you trust Him to watch over you? Do you believe that anything is possible with Him?

That can be tough sometimes. But remember this: Abraham believed God. And God's promises came true. They always do.

Help me be like Abraham:
Help me believe in You;
Help me know that Your promises
Always will come true.

## Night night, God.

Put your name in the blank and say the following sentence out loud: _____ believed the Lord.

# Your Shield, Your Reward

"Do not be afraid, Abram. I am your
shield, your very great reward."

—GENESIS 15:1 NIV

Do you ever get a little scared at night? Or during a
big, booming thunderstorm? Or *any* time at all?

It's okay. We *all* do. That's why over and over in
the Bible, we find the words, "Do not be afraid." God
says it in Genesis, the first book of the Bible, all the way
through Revelation, the last book.

God says it to people who are scared about their future. He says it to people going on a great adventure. He says it sometimes when people are just a little unsure about themselves.

So no matter why you're afraid, God has a message for you: don't be.

He tells Abraham that not only will He be his shield, his protector, but He will also be his "very great reward." In God, we have no reason to fear. He will protect us from whatever we're afraid of, and He and His goodness will also be a reward to us.

Be brave, little one. The God of the universe is your shield.

Thank You, God, for reminding me,
"Do not be afraid."
I know that You're watching over me,
Whatever comes my way.

## Night night, God.

What makes you the most afraid? Talk to God about it right now.

# Is Anything Too Hard?

"Is anything too hard for the LORD?"

—GENESIS 18:14 NIV

How many times have you said, "I can't. That's too hard"?

Well, for God, the answer is, "Never!"

But if you're a human—especially a *little* human—a lot of things can seem like you just *can't*. I can't clean that messy ol' room. I can't be nice to my brother *again*. I can't remember to brush my teeth *every* day. And sometimes things get even harder than that.

The good news is that our God is a powerful God. And nothing is too hard for Him.

When things are hard, when we think we can't, there is something we *can* do. We can always go to Him for help. And He will always listen.

Is anything too hard for the Lord? Absolutely not.

When I want to scream, "I can't!"
When things get hard to do,
Help me to remember, Lord,
That I can call on You!

Night night, God.

What is one thing that you just can't do? See what God says about that.

# God Is There

"I am with you and will watch
over you wherever you go."

—GENESIS 28:15 NIV

**T**hink about a time when you felt really lonely. Or
sad. Or afraid.

Picture it in your mind. What were you doing? How
did you feel? What could you see?

Keep that picture in your mind. But now *add God*. Whatever God looks like to you—add Him to the picture of the lonely, sad, or scary time in your mind.

Feel His warmth. Imagine His power. Know His presence.

Because *He is there.*

Every single time that you are lonely, sad, or afraid, remember that He is there. He is really, truly there with you and watching over you, whatever you do, wherever you go.

With You, God, I'm not lonely;
There is no need to fear.
No matter where I go, I know
You are always near.

Night night, God.

Close your eyes and imagine God with you right now. He is there.

# Joseph, the Dreamer

They said to each other, "Here comes that dreamer."

—Genesis 37:19

Joseph was pretty much a nobody to his brothers. Out of the twelve boys in his family, Joseph was number eleven, next to the last. And when you're the littlest, youngest person around, it can seem like everyone is bigger than you, smarter than you, and gets to do way more stuff than you.

But Joseph didn't let that bother him. Even though he was one of the littlest guys in his family, Joseph had the biggest dreams.

He would tell all of his brothers about his big dreams, but they would get mad. "Do you *really* think that's gonna happen?" they'd ask with a laugh. But Joseph kept on dreaming his dreams.

What everyone didn't know is that God had put those big dreams in Joseph's little heart. And one day, when everyone least expected it, God was going to make all of those dreams come true.

So no matter how small you are, no matter how small you *feel*, listen for the great big dreams that God has placed in your heart. When you do, you can be sure God will help those dreams come true.

God, I know I'm little,
But I know I'm growing too!
When You put dreams in my heart,
I know they will come true!

## Night night, God.

What do you dream about doing one day?

# Turning into Good

You meant to hurt me. But God
turned your evil into good.

—GENESIS 50:20

Sometimes people are mean to us. Sometimes things happen that make us feel bad. We don't always know why bad things happen. And we usually can't control it when they do. But the good news is that we can control how we *act* when bad things happen to us.

When Joseph's brothers were really mean to him, Joseph could have been really mean right back. After a

while, Joseph went from being the little brother to one of the most powerful men in Egypt. And when Joseph's brothers came begging to buy food, Joseph could've easily told them no.

But he didn't. He forgave them. He hugged them. And he took care of them. Even though Joseph's brothers tried to hurt him, he knew that God had worked it all out for the good of everyone.

When someone is mean to you, are you mean right back to them? Do you stay mad at them for a long time? Or do you forgive them and trust God to take care of the rest?

Let's forgive and see what God can do.

Dear God, when bad things happen,
I put my trust in You.
I know You can turn bad to good,
And I know You'll see me through.

## Night night, God.

Tell God about something bothering you. Trust Him to take care of you.

# Splitting the Sea

The Lord will fight for you.

—Exodus 14:14

The story of Moses parting the Red Sea is one of the most amazing miracles in the Bible. And the point of the story seems to be summed up perfectly in Exodus 14:14.

*God will fight for you.*

For Adam and Eve, it was grace. For Noah, it was telling him how to build a big boat. And for the Israelites, God's chosen people, it was two big walls of water creating a safe walkway through the Red Sea.

For me and you, who knows what it will look like?
A butterfly may flutter by just when you're feeling sad.
A warm wind may wrap you in a big ol' hug. Or, you
never know, God may have a great big water-wall of a
miracle waiting just for you.

All through the Bible, God fought for His people. He
loved them. He cared for them. And He will fight for *you*.

When there looks like no way out,
When I'm feeling blue,
I'll remember these five words:
*God will fight for you!*

## Night night, God.

Do you remember a time
when God fought for you?

# What If?

God said, "I will be with you."

—Exodus 3:12

When you think about Moses, what do you see? A man with a long white beard standing tall and holding a staff as walls of water shoot into the sky and all the people are saved! Right? The man is a hero!

But did you know that when God first called Moses to help, he wasn't so heroic?

He sounded more like . . . well, like you and me! He made excuse after excuse as to why he couldn't do what

God was asking him to do. He listed every "what if" he could think of. He thought of every reason why he couldn't be a hero for God. And do you know what God told him? "I will be with you."

In the end, Moses *is* a hero. Not because he was brave. Not because he was strong. But because God was with him. And He will be with you too.

God, when You tell me to go,
To be what You want me to be,
I know that I'll be ready 'cause
I know You'll be with me!

## Night night, God.

What do you want to do when you grow up? What do you think you could do right now?

# Who Is Like You?

Who is like You, O Lord?

—Exodus 15:11 NKJV

Once Moses and the Israelites were safe from the mean pharaoh and all his men, they looked back over the Red Sea. And suddenly, they broke out in song.

"The Lord gives me strength . . .
He has saved me.
He is my God,
And I will praise him." (Exodus 15:2)

They had seen for themselves how powerful God was and how much He loved His people. They had seen every little droplet of water in the Red Sea obey the one true God. They had seen, with their own eyes, a miracle.

Then they asked the question, "Who is like You, O Lord?" But they already knew the answer. And I'm guessing you do too.

Who is like You, Lord?

No one. Nope. *No one.*

Who is like You, Lord?
Who else can part the sea?
Who else would send a miracle
To rescue even me?

## Night night, God.

Make up your own song about God. Then sing it to someone.

# Your Promise

You keep your loving promise.

—Exodus 15:13

Have you ever made a promise to someone? Have you ever *broken* a promise to someone? Of course. We're human, and things happen that we can't control. Sometimes we're not able to do that thing we said we would.

But lucky for us, God is *not* human. God is God, and He controls everything—everything in this world, everything in this universe, and everything beyond.

Over and over in the Bible, we see God's promises come true. Sometimes they come true right away. Sometimes it takes years and years for His people to see His promises.

But one thing is for sure: when God makes a promise, He's going to keep it. And that means everything He tells us through His Word is true. Everything He promises us, we can count on.

God makes promises to us out of His great love. And He always keeps His promises.

Oh, God, thank You
For all that You say and do!
Oh, God, thank You that
Your promises come *true*!

## Night night, God.

Can you think of one of God's promises? How did it come true?

# Honor Your Parents

"Honor your father and your mother."

—Exodus 20:12

God gave Moses ten big rules for His people to follow called the Ten Commandments. He thought they were so important that He carved those rules on two big stone tablets Himself. One of the top ten rules was—you guessed it—"Honor your father and your mother."

What does it mean to honor someone? Is it respecting them? Obeying them? Showing them that you love them and care about them? Letting them know how special they are to you?

Yes. Yes. Yes, yes, yes.

Moms and dads love us more than anybody else on this planet. They take care of us. They feed us. They buy us beds and blankets and clothes and shoes and toothpaste and toys. They try to teach us to do what is right. They try to keep us safe. Every. Single. Day. And sometimes we don't make it easy on them. (Sorry, Mom and Dad.)

God created us. He made families. And He knows that honoring Mom and Dad is good for us. And it's good for them. Everyone wins when we honor our father and mother.

Thank You for my mom and dad;
They teach me who I should be.
Help me honor them every day
For all they do for me!

## Night night, God.

What are some ways that you can honor your mom and dad?

# Time for Rest

"But the seventh day is a day of
rest to honor the Lord your God."

—Exodus 20:10

In God's ten big rules, He tells us to take one day, the seventh day, to rest. After the all-powerful God created the whole wide universe, *He* rested. And He asks us to do the same.

It sounds like an easy rule, right? How hard is it to sit back and take it easy? As silly as it sounds, we have a lot of trouble with this one! Right now, do you want to rest? Or can you think of a bazillion other things that you'd rather be doing?

But we have to remember that God created us. He dreamed up all the pieces and parts of our bodies, and He put them together. He knows how the human body works. And He knows that with rest, we'll all be our best.

The seventh day, the sabbath day, is a holy day. It's a day to think about God, to worship Him, and to think about all of the wonderful things that He's done in our lives. *And to rest.*

We can't really focus on God if we're running around doing all kinds of busy-ness. Can we?

Just rest. Then watch and see how God makes you your best.

Thank You, God, for reminding me
To stop and take a rest;
I know that when I rest in You,
I'll always be my best!

## Night night, God.

Why do you think rest is good for you?

# Love Your Neighbor

"Love your neighbor as
you love yourself."

—Leviticus 19:18

God gave His people a lot of very important rules. He gave us rules to keep us happy and healthy. He gave us rules to keep us safe and secure. And He gave us rules about how to treat other people, so that they, too, can be happy and healthy, safe and secure.

One of those rules that we see over and over—at least ten times in the Bible—is to love your neighbor as yourself. You may have heard it before at church or in the Bible. But have you thought about what it really means to love your neighbor as yourself?

How do you treat yourself? Do you hurt yourself? No. So let's be careful not to hurt others. Do you want to go first on the slide? Yes! So maybe let someone else go first on the slide. Do you want the biggest brownie for yourself? Yes! So (at least every once in a while) give the biggest brownie to your brother.

Whether you're on the playground, at the grocery store, or in your own home, think about how other people feel. Think about how you would like to be treated. Then love that other person like yourself.

When I'm not sure how to act,
What to do, or what to say,
I'll just treat others like myself
And let love lead the way!

## Night night, God.

What is one way that you could show love to someone else?

# God of Mercy

The Lord your God is a merciful God.

—DEUTERONOMY 4:31

**E**ven if we try and try to follow the rules God gave us, we're still going to mess up. A lot. And that's okay.

The Bible tells us that God is merciful. It means that even though we mess up, He still loves us—no matter what. It means that even though He knows our mistakes, He also knows the good inside our hearts. It means that even though our sin deserves death, He offers us a life forever with Him.

So when you mess up, don't hide. Don't blame it on someone else. Take it to God. Tell Him that you're sorry. And He will show you His mercy and His love.

God, thank You for Your mercy;
Thank You for Your love;
Thank You for Your gift of grace—
I know these are enough.

## Night night, God.

How have you messed up lately? Tell God about it.

# With Everything

"Love the Lord your God with all
your heart, soul and strength."

—Deuteronomy 6:5

How much do you love your favorite stuffed animal or your favorite food? How much do you love your mom and your dad?

Even as much as you love all of those things, God

wants you to love Him even *more*. Do you? Can you? Will you?

God loves you. He created you. And He loves you more than you could ever imagine.

He wants you to love Him with everything you have—with all your heart, all your soul, and all your strength. And since He gave you everything you have, why not love Him with everything that you have?

Dear God, I love You more than
There are fishes in the sea,
But there's no way that I could love You
More than You love me!

## Night night, God.

What is one way that you can show your love for God?

# A Donkey Talks

I have stood here to stop you.
What you are doing is wrong.

—NUMBERS 22:32

Think about how many choices you make every day. What to wear. What to do. What to say. Every moment of every day!

Some choices are pretty easy. Like, do I want to wear my cowboy boots? Of course! But some are tougher. Like, should I listen to my mom, or do I listen to my friends?

Hmm, probably Mom. When you're little and learning—even when you're older and know better!—sometimes it's hard to know exactly which way is the *right* way.

When Balaam was going the wrong way, an angel of God came down to tell him so. God even made Balaam's *donkey* talk so that he could tell Balaam what he was doing wrong. Only then did Balaam stop and talk to God about where he was going.

When it comes time for us to choose, we may not have angels or donkeys talking to us like Balaam did. But we do have parents and the Bible and that little feeling inside to help us know right from wrong. Let's listen and choose the path God has for us.

Dear God, sometimes it's hard
To know which way is right;
Help me always to follow
Your leading, guiding light.

Night night, God.

Have you ever turned away from a wrong choice? What happened?

# Strong and Brave

"Remember that I commanded
you to be strong and brave."

—Joshua 1:9

ho needs a reminder sometimes to be strong and
brave? (I'm raising my hand way up high!)

Things wear you out. Things change. Things get scary! And in the middle of all of those things, we sometimes need a little reminder.

Joshua had a lot of scary things going on. Moses, the leader of God's people, had just died. And God made Joshua the new leader. Joshua was supposed to lead all of the Israelites into the land God had promised them. *But how?!*

That's when God sent His reminder: "Just as I was with Moses, so I will be with you. . . . Be strong and brave" (Joshua 1:5, 7).

Just as God was with Moses and Joshua—and every other great leader in the Bible—He will be with you too.

God, when things get scary,
I know just what I'll do!
I'll remember Your reminder:
"I will be with you!"

## Night night, God.

Close your eyes. Feel God's presence making you strong and brave.

# Joshua and the Big Wall

"Then the walls of the city will fall."

—Joshua 6:5

Joshua stood strong and brave. He looked at the big wall keeping God's people from the promised land. "Okay, God, now what?" he asked. Then God gave Joshua some very specific instructions. Joshua followed them, and the wall fell!

It sounds *so* simple, doesn't it? "Do this, and the walls of the city will fall."

But the instructions didn't sound like they would work. And Joshua had to get a *lot* of people to follow them. And God's people didn't really know what was waiting for them on the other side.

But it really *was* that simple. Following God's instructions got God's people to where they wanted to go. It worked for Joshua. And it will work for you and me.

Which way, God?
I know You know the way.
If You'll tell me where to go,
I promise to obey.

## Night night, God.

What is one direction that you know God wants you to follow?

# Serve the Lord

"As for me and my family,
we will serve the Lord."

—Joshua 24:15

Once God's people got to the promised land, Joshua
sat them all down, and they had a little talk. Joshua
reminded the people of everything that God had done for

them, of all the many ways that God had helped His people get to where they were.

Then Joshua told them to choose. "You must decide whom you will serve" (Joshua 24:15). Joshua let them know loud and clear, "As for me and my family, we will serve the Lord."

Whether we think about it or not, serving God is a choice that we make every single day. Every single *minute* of every single day. Are we serving God with our thoughts, our time, and our actions? Or are we serving something else?

Right now, reading this devotional, I'd say you're choosing to serve the Lord! And that, my friend, is a wonderful choice.

Dear God, there is no one
Who could love me like You do;
So when I choose whom to serve,
Of course I choose You!

## Night night, God.

What is one way that you can choose to serve the Lord?

# The Wimpy Warrior

The Lord is with you, mighty warrior!

—Judges 6:12

When Gideon felt small, weak, and helpless, an angel called him "mighty." The angel reminded Gideon that maybe things weren't as bad as they seemed. He reminded Gideon that God was still with him.

And for Gideon, that made all the difference. Knowing that God was on his side, Gideon stepped out bravely into his role as a mighty warrior.

Sometimes we all feel a little small, a little weak, or a little helpless. And sometimes we just need to remember *who we are*.

Who is that person in your life? Who is the one always reminding you how smart you are, how strong you are, and how unbelievably loved by God you are? Be thankful for that person today. And try to be that person to someone else.

God is with us. And that makes us *all* mighty warriors.

Hey, look at my muscles,
So big and oh so strong!
I knew that You were with me, God,
Here with me all along!

## Night night, God.

How does God make you feel mighty?

# God Calls Samuel

Samuel said, "Speak, Lord. I am
your servant, and I am listening."

—1 SAMUEL 3:10

O kay, let's be honest. How many of you have ever said,
out loud, "Speak, Lord. I am listening"?

Yeah, me neither.

But imagine if we did. Imagine if we not only said it out
loud *one* day, but if we said it in our minds and in our hearts
*every* day. What if we said it every time we made a little
choice? Or a big decision? What if we lived our lives always
listening for the voice and direction of God?

You've already met a lot of heroes from
the Bible. You know what happened

when they listened and obeyed. Just imagine what could happen with us.

Say it with me now, "Speak, Lord. I am listening." And repeat it, deep in your hearts, in your minds, out loud, shouted from the rooftops, every single day, from here on out. I can't wait to see what God will do.

Speak, Lord, I am listening,
To Your Word, to what You say.
Speak, Lord, I am listening,
Every moment, every day.

# Night night, God.

Listen. What do you think God is saying?

# The Great Big Meanie

I come to you in the name
of the LORD All-Powerful.

—1 SAMUEL 17:45 NCV

Like Gideon, David was the smallest guy in his family. But unlike Gideon, nobody reminded David that he was a mighty warrior. In fact, when that mean ol' Goliath came along, everybody told David that he was too young, too small, and didn't have enough experience to fight a warrior like Goliath.

It was okay, though, because nobody *needed* to remind David that he was mighty. He knew that the power of God was inside of him. He had already seen it at work! As a shepherd, he had stood bravely against whatever animal came around to threaten his sheep, and he won every time.

So when that big bully Goliath came out to threaten the army of God's people, David knew he could take him down, even if everyone else was scared of him. He knew that even the youngest, smallest kid with no experience could win if God was on his side.

And you know what? David was right. He stood up for God. And God stood up for him.

God, thank You for helping me to
Stand up for what is right.
I know that You will fight for me,
With all Your power, all Your might!

## Night night, God.

How does God fight for you?

# The World's Wisest King

I ask that you give me a
heart that understands.

—1 KINGS 3:9 NCV

If you could have anything in the world, what would you ask for? Money? A new bike? Chocolate cupcakes with rainbow sprinkles?

King Solomon had the chance to ask God for

anything he wanted. And you know what he asked for? Wisdom, understanding, and guidance in leading God's people. Instead of asking for something for himself, Solomon asked for something that served God. That would be really hard to do!

But it worked out pretty well for King Solomon, didn't it? God was happy with what Solomon asked for, so He gave him wisdom, *plus* a lot of things he didn't ask for! Solomon became known as the richest, wisest king in the world. And we're still talking about his wisdom today.

God, just like Solomon,
Give me a heart that understands.
Help me to know what is best;
Let me be Your helping hand.

## Night night, God.

What has God already given you? How can you use it to help His people?

# The World's Bravest Queen

Who knows, you may have been chosen
queen for just such a time as this.

—Esther 4:14

God chose you. Did you know that? Jesus said it right here in John 15:16: "You did not choose me; I chose you."

God chose Moses to lead His people out of Egypt. He chose Joshua to lead them into the promised land. He chose David to take down Goliath. He chose Esther to save her people.

What did He choose you for? What is that unique thing He has planned for you? It doesn't have to be a great big miracle that you're forever famous for. It can be as simple as being a friend everyone can count on. It can be using your imagination to solve big problems. It can be using your words to tell the world about Jesus.

If you don't know what it is, that's perfectly okay. Just keep seeking God and being obedient to Him, and you'll step right into the role that you were forever meant to play . . . for such a time as this.

God, I can't imagine why
You'd choose little ol' me,
But I'm thankful and I'm ready
To be who You want me to be!

Night night, God.

What do you think
you've been chosen for?
Talk to God about it.

# You Keep Me Safe

I go to bed and sleep in peace.
Lord, only you keep me safe.

—PSALM 4:8

When you go to bed at night, what do you do?
Turn on the nightlight? Check under the bed?
Shut the closet door? Pull the covers over your head?

But none of those things really keeps you safe, does
it? It can help you see better. It can make you feel better.
But really, if you're wanting to feel safe and secure,
you have a much more powerful force *already* at work,
watching over you.

You guessed it. "Lord, only you keep me safe."

So tonight, nightlight or not, you can go to sleep in peace. Rest and know that the Lord, the Creator of the universe and everything in it, is right there, keeping you safe.

I know You keep me safe
When I'm home or I'm away.
I know You're watching over me,
Every night and every day.

## Night night, God.

What makes you feel safe?

# When Trouble Comes

God is our protection and our strength.
He always helps in times of trouble.

—Psalm 46:1

How was your day today? Was it full of sunshine and fun? Was it stormy and awful? Or was it a little bit of sunshine and rain?

We're going to have troubles in this world. It's a fact. But good or bad, sunshine or rain, God is there to help. Always.

This psalm says that He is "our protection and our strength." He is not only watching over us and protecting us, but He is also making us stronger. He will give us the strength to play in the sunshine *and* to withstand the storms.

No matter what comes our way, let's thank Him for the sunshiny days and hold tightly to Him through the storms.

Dear God, when trouble comes,
I know I can count on You;
I know You're always with me,
And I know You'll help me through.

## Night night, God.

Tell God about any troubles you're having.

# Rejoice and Be Glad!

This is the day that the Lord
has made. Let us rejoice
and be glad today!

—Psalm 118:24

**B**irthdays! Play days! Getting-new-toy days! Those are days to celebrate! Right?!

But what about sick days? Skinned-my-knee days? Running-errands-all-day days? Those days . . . well, they're a little harder to celebrate.

But Psalm 118:24 reminds us that *every* day is a day that God made. *Every* day is a day to "rejoice and be glad."

So on those sick days, maybe we can be happy for a comfy bed to rest in. Skinned knees? Let's be grateful for someone who kisses those boo-boos. Running errands? Think of all the cool stuff you'll see along the way!

Just keep looking, and I know that you can find joy in *each and every* day! Because *every* day is a day that the Lord has made.

Sad days and rainy days,
Days with nothing to do—
I will look for joy in them
Because they're made by You!

Night night, God.

What was something awesome about today?

# God Never Sleeps

He who guards you never sleeps.

—Psalm 121:3

**W**hat's the latest you've ever stayed up? And how did you feel the next day? Tired? Grumpy? Like you never wanted to get out of bed ever again?

Our bodies were made to sleep. We were made to need rest. We go and go all day, and then finally, our bodies get to do nothing for a while so that they can recharge.

But did you know that God *never* sleeps? Sure, He rested on the seventh day. He took a little break after creating the *entire universe*. But He is always on guard, always watching over you, over this earth.

So when it's time for your little body and your big brain to take a break, rest easy. And know that the God who loves you and protects you *never* sleeps.

God, tonight I'll go to bed,
Close my eyes, not make a peep,
Because I know You're watching me,
Yes, even as I sleep.

# Night night, God.

What do you think
God is doing right now?

# Amazing Me!

I praise you because you made me
in an amazing and wonderful way.

—Psalm 139:14

Look at you! Just *look* at you!
Look at those beautiful eyes. And that gorgeous
hair. And those cute little toes. It doesn't get any cuter
than *you*!

Plus, there's that brain in your head, thinking up the
most wonderful thoughts. There's also that strong heart
in your chest, *beat, beat, beat*-ing up a rhythm. And then

there are those lungs that keep breathing air in and out all day long.

Think about how absolutely amazing you are. God made you that way, you know. He made you "in an amazing and wonderful way." The Bible says so, right there in black and white.

So anytime you start thinking that you're not smart enough or cute enough, that you're *not* amazing or wonderful—I'm sorry, but you're wrong. Because God made you, and He made you in an *amazing* and *wonderful* way.

Thank You, God, for creating
The most amazing *me*—
Wonderfully made, exactly how
You wanted me to be!

## Night night, God.

What is one amazingly wonderful thing about yourself?

# Heart Healer

[God] heals the brokenhearted.

—Psalm 147:3

There are things that happen in this life that don't seem fair, things we can't explain, things that make our hearts so sad that we don't know what to do.

We may lose a pet or a grandparent, or a best friend may move away. Maybe it's just a part of life. But what do we *do* with those parts of life?

We take them to God. We lean on God's promises. We put our trust in Him. And when we do, Psalm 147:3 tells us that He will heal our broken hearts.

Most of the time, this life is a wonderful, beautiful

thing. But when it's not, know that there's One who can heal a broken heart.

He is the One who put your heart together in the first place. And He can certainly put it back together again.

Dear God, when I'm really sad,
Please heal my broken heart;
I know You can put back in place
All the broken parts.

## Night night, God.

How does God make you feel better when you're sad?

# Star Counter

[God] counts the stars
and names each one.

—Psalm 147:4

It's kind of hard to imagine what God is like—just how big, how awesome, how powerful, how loving He is.

The Bible gives us a lot of details if we look. And one detail is this: He counts the stars. He names each one.

Can you imagine?! Try to count the stars. It's impossible!

But not for your God. Not only has He counted every single star, but He knows every single one by name. Think about that for a minute.

And think about this: if He cares to personally number and name the stars—those big, floating balls of gas—imagine how much He cares about you.

God, I can't imagine
Just how great You are;
And yet I know You care for me
Even more than all the stars.

## Night night, God.

Go ahead. Try to count the stars.

# Trust the Lord

Trust the Lord with all your heart.

—PROVERBS 3:5

"Trust the Lord." We hear this proverb a lot, don't we? But what exactly does it mean? And what exactly does it look like if you trust in Him?

Well, for starters, trusting in Him is believing in Him. Wouldn't you say? Trusting in Him is knowing that what He says is true. Trusting in Him is knowing that He *can* do what He says He can do. And He *will* do what He says He will do.

So what does that mean for you and me? How does that affect the way we live?

First, we would want to learn a lot about Him. We would want to know more about what He says and what He can do and will do. We can do that by reading our Bibles and spending time with Him.

And then we would need to believe—believe in the words He's written for us, believe in the prayers He's listening to, believe that He's loving us and working in our lives, even though we can't see Him.

He loves you. He cares for you. He wants your trust, with your whole heart.

God, I want to know You,
To learn to trust in You,
To believe in You with my whole heart,
To know You love me too.

## Night night, God.

What is one thing that you know about God?

# Love Forgives All

Love forgives all wrongs.

—Proverbs 10:12

**W**hat's the worst, meanest, most horrible thing anyone has ever done to you? How do you feel about it now? Are you still mad about it? Hurt? Sad?

It's okay to feel all of those feelings. But sooner or later (sooner is better), we have to forgive.

Proverbs 10:12 reminds us that love forgives *all* wrongs. And it's not just the wrongs that are kind of bad. It's not just the wrongs done by people who love us. It's not just the wrongs that are followed with an "I'm sorry." It says *all* wrongs.

*All* is a big word. It's a scary word. It's a word that, in this case, means you can't stay mad forever. Do you know why? It's not good to stay mad forever. It's not good *for you*.

So let's take a lesson from love today and forgive all wrongs. All of them. Give them to God, and let Him cover those wrongs with His love.

Dear God, I'm really sorry
For staying mad so long.
I forgive all, as You do me
When I do something wrong.

Night night, God.

Who is someone that you need to forgive?

# Prince of Peace

A child will be born to us.
God will give a son to us.

—Isaiah 9:6

**W**hen was the last time you had to wait for something you really, really wanted? A vacation? A birthday party? A new baby brother?

For years and *years*, God's people heard the promise of

Isaiah 9:6. God's prophet Isaiah told it to God's people. Then they told it to their children and grandchildren and *their* grandchildren.

Can you imagine how excited they were? Can you imagine what it was like to wait for that long for something so wonderful?

God's people had some tough times while they were waiting. Some had to move far away from home. Some lost their families. Some had to be servants and slaves.

But through it all, they waited with the hope that a Savior was coming—a "Powerful God," a "Father Who Lives Forever," and once and for all, a "Prince of Peace" (Isaiah 9:6).

Dear God, while I'm waiting,
I'll keep my hope in You;
I know You've promised good, good things,
And Your promises are true.

## Night night, God.

What are you waiting for?

# Strong Again

The people who trust the Lord
will become strong again.

—Isaiah 40:31

et me see your muscles. Ooh, nice!

Okay, now let me see your spiritual muscles. You
know, your faith muscles, your I-believe-in-God muscles.

It's a little harder to show those muscles, huh? But we do. We show them in our everyday lives with the choices we make, how we treat other people, and the way we act and feel when trouble comes our way.

Isaiah 40:31 reminds us that our trust in the Lord will make us strong. When we feel weak, when we feel tired, we remember our trust in the Lord—the way He's always with us, fighting for us. And we will be strong again.

God, I know when I am weak,
You will make me strong again;
When my muscles are feeling small,
I know who my trust is in!

Night night, God.

How are your faith muscles feeling right now?

# Your God

"Don't be afraid, because
I am your God."

—Isaiah 41:10

It's just the wind."

"This won't hurt a bit."

"There's nothing to be afraid of."

These are all things people say when they don't want us to be afraid. But does it really work?

What if instead we turn to the truth that is truer than true? Don't be afraid. Why? Because He is your God. Plain and simple.

When you're scared, is there anything that helps more than knowing that the Creator of the entire universe is yours? *He is your God.*

Here for you. Watching over you. Listening to you. Loving you.

And knowing that, there really is no reason to be afraid.

God, when the wind is howling
And shadows are closing in,
I'll remember that You're my God,
And I'll be brave again!

Night night, God.

Think for a moment about how big and powerful your God is.

# Good Plans

"I know what I have planned
for you," says the Lord. "I
have good plans for you."

—Jeremiah 29:11

**W**hat are your plans for tomorrow? Big plans? Little plans? *Any* plans?

Did you know that God has plans for you too?

Long ago when God's people were going through some really tough times, He reminded them of this. Through His prophet Jeremiah, God told His people that He had plans for them beyond the tough times. His plans were good plans, plans to give them a good future.

Whether you're going through tough times or not, God has good plans for you too. We may not know exactly what those plans are, but if God says that they're good, you can believe that they are. Keep your eye on Him, and His plans will happen in your life too.

God, I'm so excited,
And I can't wait to see
All the good things You have waiting,
The plans You have for me.

Night night, God.

What kind of plans are you making right now?

# A Brand-New Day

The Lord's love never ends.
His mercies never stop. They
are new every morning.

—Lamentations 3:22-23

Was your day awesomely awesome? Awfully awful? Somewhere in between?

No matter how you answered, it's all good. Do you know why? God's mercies are new every morning.

That doesn't really mean that you have to wait until morning for God to show you His mercy. But like the verse says, "His mercies never stop." He is merciful all the time.

No matter how awfully awful something is, you can take it to God. He will show you His mercy.

So think again about your day today. If it was awesomely awesome or anywhere in between, thank God for the wonderful day that you had. If it was awfully awful, talk to God about it. Let Him cover it in His mercy and grace.

Thank You, God, that Your mercies
Are brand new every day;
I know Your mercies never stop—
Whatever comes my way!

Night night, God.

Talk to God about your day today.

# Daniel Is Safe

God saved Daniel from the
power of the lions.

—Daniel 6:27

There are many Bible verses about God keeping us safe. But they're not just Bible verses. They're not just words on a piece of paper. They are the truth of the powerful, living God. And Daniel knew that.

So when some mean men made a rule that said Daniel couldn't pray to God, Daniel prayed to God anyway. Daniel knew that he was doing nothing wrong. In fact, he was doing what was *right*. And he knew that God would keep him safe.

And that's exactly what happened. Even though Daniel was thrown into a den full of lions, even though it seemed impossible that he would make it out of there, God kept Daniel safe.

God, I know Your promise
To keep me safe is true;
And I will trust Your promises
Like Daniel trusted You.

## Night night, God.

What do you think Daniel was thinking in the lions' den?

# Jonah Doesn't Obey (at First)

Lord, I prayed to you. And
you heard my prayers.

—Jonah 2:7

Jonah had messed up. Big time. God had asked him
to do something, and Jonah ran the other way.

Raise your hand if you've ever messed up. Yeah, me too. And everyone else on this planet.

Don't you think that's why we have the story of Jonah? Along with all of these other amazing people of faith, we also have stories of people who didn't get it right, stories of people who messed up big time. And God loved them anyway.

In the story of Jonah, he finally prayed to God. He told God that he was sorry. And God heard his prayers. Even after he'd messed up. Even in the dark, yucky belly of a big fish.

God hears us. And He loves us anyway.

Dear God, when I mess up,
Thank You for being there;
Thank You for reminding me that
You'll hear me *anywhere*!

## Night night, God.

Imagine being in the belly of a big fish. What would it look like, feel like, and smell like?

# Rest in His Love

You will rest in [God's] love. He will
sing and be joyful about you.

—ZEPHANIAH 3:17

What is your favorite lullaby? You know, the song that always helps you fall asleep at night. Is it something classic, like "Lullaby and Goodnight"? Is it "Jesus Loves Me"? Or is it simply the hum of a fan or the chirping of birds outside your window?

Whatever it is, I've got a new one for you. It's God's lullaby. Did you know that He sings about you? He does! You make Him happy, and He sings songs about you.

You can rest in that. You can rest in that joy. You can rest in His love.

Tonight, as you are drifting off to sleep, listen for God's lullaby. You may not hear it with your ears. But if you listen really closely, you can hear it with your heart.

Dear God, I love to hear You
Singing over me with love;
I know the sweetest lullabies
Are the ones from up above.

## Night night, God.

What do you think God's lullaby says about you?

# Devotions from the New Testament

# An Angel Visits Mary and Joseph

God can do everything!

—LUKE 1:37

When God decided to save the world by sending His Son, He didn't just—*whoosh*—send Jesus down to earth as a full-grown man. He could have. But He didn't.

Instead, He sent the angel Gabriel to a girl in a small village. "God chose you, Mary. You're going to be the mother of God's own Son."

*But how? Why?* Mary had lots of questions. And they had one simple answer: "God can do everything!"

And that was enough for Mary. She didn't know exactly how it would happen. She didn't know exactly why. But she knew that she trusted God.

And that He would and could do everything to save His people.

So Mary said yes. And she is now forever a part of the story that saved the world.

Dear God, I don't know exactly
What Your plans for me will bring,
But I do know one thing for sure:
You can do anything!

Night night, God.

If you could do anything, what would you do?

# A Miracle in a Stable

Today your Savior was
born in David's town.

—Luke 2:11

A King had just been born. He wasn't just any king. He was the King of all kings.

But when the angels came to announce it, they didn't fly from castle to castle, telling all the royal families that the new King was here. No. They went to an open field, full of dirty sheep watched by smelly shepherds.

Some people thought that shepherds were kind of weird. Some people thought that shepherds were kind of dangerous. But God thought that shepherds were exactly the kind of people He wanted to tell about His Son's arrival on earth.

So right there in that open field, those wandering men were some of the first to learn about God's own Son. It was a life-changing message for them that night. And it is a life-changing message for us tonight.

*Your Savior has been born.*

Dear God, thank You for sending
Your Son to us on earth;
That very night the world was changed,
With this one baby's birth.

Night night, God.

What does Jesus'
birth mean to you?

# Angels in the Sky

Then the shepherds went back
to their sheep, praising God and
thanking him for everything that
they had seen and heard.

—LUKE 2:20

**W**hen the shepherds heard that the Savior was born,
first they went to see for themselves. And it was

just as the angels had said: a newborn, lying in a manger, wrapped in soft cloths. It was Him. It was God's own Son. And they had seen Him with their own eyes.

After that, knowing the news was true, they did two things: They praised God. Then they thanked Him.

It's a pretty good example for us to follow too. God does so many amazing things for us. Even after the ultimate gift of sending His Son, He continues to give us gifts that bring joy to our lives. For all of these things, we can praise Him and thank Him, just as the shepherds did.

How can I say thank You, God,
For all that You've done for me?
I'll just keep praising You and thanking You
For all eternity!

## Night night, God.

What has God done for you?

# Jesus in His Father's House

Jesus said to them, "Why were you
looking for me? Didn't you know that
I must be in my Father's house?"

—LUKE 2:49 NCV

As a twelve-year-old, Jesus was already wise beyond
His years. When His parents lost track of Him on

a trip to Jerusalem, His reply was so simple. "Didn't you already know where I'd be?"

We might think the same thing when we read that story. "Why didn't they check the temple, His Father's house?"

How about you now in your own life? Where do *you* look when you're looking for Jesus? Where can we find Him? He is as real today as He was when He was a twelve-year-old boy. We just have to know where to look to find Him.

He's in the Bible, God's Word to us. He's in the godly wisdom of our parents. And yes, He is still right there, in His Father's house.

Dear Jesus, I can see You
Everywhere I look,
Especially in Your Father's house
And in the pages of His book.

## Night night, Jesus.

Where is your favorite place to hide?

# Follow, Follow Me!

"Come and follow me. I will make
you fishermen for men."

—Mark 1:17

When Jesus chose His disciples long, long ago, He told them they were going to fish for people. Did that mean they were going to put a worm on a hook and throw it at people walking by? That would probably be funny, but that's not what Jesus was talking about.

Jesus meant that He and His disciples, His helpers, would go out and bring people into God's kingdom, just as fishermen would bring fish into their boats. It would be hard work. It might be stinky work. But it would be the most important work.

And even though Jesus said those words a long time ago, He still needs disciples today. He still wants us to go out and tell people about Him. And He wants us to help other people learn about the kingdom of God. He still needs us to be fishers of men.

Dear Jesus, I am ready
To help You fish for men;
Lead me, guide me, show me the way;
Show me where to begin.

Night night, Jesus.

How can we help
Jesus fish for people?

# Make Peace

"Those who work to bring
peace are happy."

—MATTHEW 5:9

Think about your day today.
Did you make someone smile? Did you
share your favorite toy? Did you solve a
problem that was making someone sad?
Did you make someone happy who
was getting mad?

If so, you can stand proud.
You are a peacemaker. And the
Bible says that peacemakers
are blessed by God.

Let's look for ways to be
peacemakers every day. Look
for a way to make someone
happy. Look for a way to
calm someone who is mad.
Look for a way to bring

joy to someone who is sad. And in doing so, we will be happier, the people around us will be happier, and we will be known as peacemakers, the children of God.

Dear God, please show me how to
Bring peace to every day;
Help me to tell about Your love
With what I do and say.

Night night, God.

What is one way that you brought peace to this day?

# Jesus Calms a Storm

"Quiet! Be still!" Then the wind
stopped, and the lake became calm.

—Mark 4:39

**W**hat do you do on your stormy days? On the days
when everything is going wrong? On the days
when it's loud and scary and you can't see what's ahead?
When Jesus and His disciples were in a boat on the
Sea of Galilee, a storm broke out. In

that moment, they showed us
two different ways that we
could act. The disciples? They
panicked. Jesus? He told the
storm to be quiet. Then He
asked His followers about their
faith.

We usually don't have control
over the stormy days. But we

can control how we act when they come. Panicking makes the storm even more crazy. But when we have faith, when we take those days to Jesus, He will calm the storm.

Jesus, sometimes I panic
When things get stormy here;
Help me always to keep my faith,
Trusting You to calm my fears.

**Night night, Jesus.**

picture one of your stormy days. Now picture Jesus saying, "Quiet! Be still!" What happens?

# God Loves You
## *So* Much

"God loved the world so much
that he gave his only Son."

—John 3:16

There's no way that we could ever measure God's love for us. Ever.

But John 3:16 gives us the biggest, best example of that love. God loved us—the whole world—so much that He gave us His Son. *His only Son.*

God sent Jesus to earth to see us and to meet us, to eat with us and to teach us, to be a living, breathing example of the best way to live. And then, even though Jesus had never done anything wrong, God allowed Jesus to die for our sins. *Because He loves us so much.*

As much as your parents and grandparents and aunts and uncles and brothers and sisters and teachers and friends love you, it doesn't even come close—even when all added up together—to how much God loves you.

I may never understand
Just why You love us so,
Even though I can't explain it:
You love me, this I know.

Night night, God.

How do you show people
that you love them?

# Whoever Believes

"God gave his Son so that
whoever believes in him may not
be lost, but have eternal life."

—John 3:16

**W**hen God gave His only Son, Jesus, to us, He took the punishment for every sin, every wrong thing ever done. He took my sins, your sins, our parents' sins, and sins for generations to come. He took it all.

He pulls us out of the darkness and into the light. He pulls us out of the mud and washes us clean. Instead of paying for our own sins with death, we are invited to a life forever with Him.

It's so difficult to understand. Why would someone love us that much? Why would a holy God care so much about humans who sin? But He does.

We can never explain it. We can never understand it. We can only say yes to the gift He has given to us, the gift for those who believe.

Jesus, I believe in You;
I know You died for me;
I know You saved me from my sins;
I know You set me free!

## Night night, Jesus.

Take a moment to talk to Jesus. Thank Him for His precious gift.

# A Boy Shares His Lunch

Here is a boy with five loaves of barley bread and two little fish.

—John 6:9

**W**hen you're little, sometimes you think that you can't help others. Sometimes you think that you can't make a difference. Sometimes you think that you're too young for God to work through you. But the story of Jesus feeding five thousand people shows us that none of that is true.

Jesus saw the thousands of people walking

toward them and suggested feeding them. That's when Philip answered, "Someone would have to work almost a year to buy enough bread for each person here to have only a little piece" (John 6:7). Only a grownup could help here, and even then, only a little bit. Right?

But Andrew spoke up and showed Jesus the boy with five loaves and two fish. It was just a little kid with a little lunch. How was that going to help?

One answer: Jesus.

We know what happened when that little boy stepped up. And we know what can happen with you. You can do big things with Jesus, every day.

Okay, Jesus, I'm all in;
Let's go do something huge!
I'm putting my life in Your hands;
Let's see what we can do!

## Night night, Jesus.

Dream about what you and Jesus could do together.

# Jesus Walks on Water

Jesus said, "Come."

—Matthew 14:29

Imagine it. You're out on the lake. In a boat. It's getting dark. You're dozing off, being gently rocked by the waves.

Suddenly you tumble down onto the floor. You open your eyes, only to squint against the spray from the waves hitting you in the face. The wind is whipping the sail. The boat is no longer gently rocking. It's bouncing wildly in the waves. You look out on the water and see something walking on the water. No,

it's some*one*. *It's Jesus.* He reaches His hand out to you.
"Come."

Do you go? Do you leave the safety of the boat to
walk with Jesus?

Well, Peter did. He went for Jesus. And he walked on
the water.

When the water's rocky,
I won't run and hide;
I'll walk in faith because I know
You'll be right by my side.

## Night night, Jesus.

What does it mean
to walk in faith?

# Jesus Heals

[Jesus] took her hand, and she stood up.

—MATTHEW 9:25

When you're sick, or hurt, or sad, what do you do? Take medicine? Put on a bandage? Go hug your mom?

All of those things are good, smart things to do. But do you think about Jesus too?

Jesus healed the lame, lepers, and little girls. He helped blind men to see. He made bad spirits come out of people. He healed people inside and out. He even brought a guy back from the dead. He can help us too.

So the next time someone is sick, hurt, or sad, sure, medicine, bandages, and hugs will help. But be

sure that you also take those hurts to Jesus. He is the
healer of them all.

Jesus, I know You healed the sick,
The sad—and a dead man too!
The next time that I'm feeling bad,
I'm taking it to You!

# Night night, Jesus.

Who needs healing right
now? Tell Jesus about them.

# Jesus Loves You

Jesus said, "Let the little
children come to me."

—Matthew 19:14

Listen. Are you listening? I need you to listen.
If you only hear one thing, if you only remember one message out of this entire book, I would say that this is the most important one.

Jesus loves you. Jesus *loves* you. Jesus. The King of kings. The Lord of lords. The Savior sent to save the world. God's own Son. He loves you.

He knows you. He gave His life for you. He knows everything about you. And He absolutely adores you.

When things get scary, remember this. When things get lonely, tell yourself this. When things get mean, *know this*.

Jesus. Loves. You.

Jesus loves me, yes, He does;
And I know that it's true.
Jesus loves me oh so much—
And, Jesus, I love You!

## Night night, Jesus.

How do you know that Jesus loves you?

# Light of the World

[Jesus] said, "I am the
light of the world."

—John 8:12

Imagine a light so bright that it looks like daytime
even when it's night.

Imagine a light so bright that even the darkest evil
cannot hide.

Imagine a light so bright that the stars and sun and moon look dark in comparison.

Jesus is that light. He is the light of the whole world. And He is here to chase away the darkness, to make evil run and hide, and to outshine even the sun.

He is a light for you and me, leading the way, showing us what's right, and helping us to see, even when everything seems dark.

Look for Jesus. Follow Him. He is the light of the world.

Jesus, I will follow You
And Your bright-shining light;
I know You'll always lead the way,
Even through the darkest night.

## Night night, Jesus.

What's the brightest light you've ever seen? Just imagine: Jesus is brighter!

# The Nice Neighbor

Jesus said to him, "Then go and
do the same thing he did!"

—LUKE 10:37

Jesus reminds us to be nice to our neighbors. But what
does that mean? What does that look like?

In His story of the Good Samaritan, it meant paying

attention, checking on someone who was having a bad day, and doing everything he could to make it better.

For you, it may be picking a flower for your mom. It may be drawing a special picture for someone in the hospital. It may be singing a song for your friend or calling to check on your granddaddy.

As we go through each day, let's keep an eye out for our neighbors, our family, and our friends. And then let's love them. Love them like the Good Samaritan did and like Jesus told us to.

Jesus, please help me to see
What my neighbors need;
Help me to love them like myself,
With my words and with my deeds.

## Night night, Jesus.

How can you show love to a neighbor?

# "If You Can"

Jesus said to the father, "You said, 'If you can!' All things are possible for him who believes."

—Mark 9:23

A man with a sick son walked up to Jesus. He told Jesus how sick his son had been and told Him how even the disciples hadn't been able to help the boy. Then the man said to Jesus, "If you can do anything for him, please have pity on us and help us" (Mark 9:22).

Can you imagine that? Saying "if You can" to Jesus?!

At this point in the story, I like to imagine the look on Jesus' face. It's the wide-eyed look your mom makes right before she puts her hands on her hips.

"'If you can!'" Jesus said, repeating the man's words. "All things are possible for him who believes."

When we ask Jesus for help, let's not make that same mistake. Let's not wonder *if* He can. Let's ask Him *knowing* that He can.

Jesus, You can do *anything*!
I know that this is true;
So whenever I need some help,
I'm coming straight to You!

## Night night, Jesus.

Do you believe? If so, what is possible for you?

# Jesus Washes Feet

"You also should wash
each other's feet."

—John 13:14

**R**aise your hand if you like washing other people's feet. Anyone? No? No one?

Now imagine washing feet in Jesus' day. Everyone walked pretty much everywhere they went. And most of the roads weren't paved. They were mostly made of dirt.

Add to that the fact that most people wore sandals . . . open toes, my friends. And you've got yourself a pretty sticky, smelly situation.

Only the lowest of the helpers had the job of washing feet. But when it came time for Jesus to leave His disciples a final message, that's what He chose to do for them. He washed their stinky, smelly feet. Then He told them, "Wash each other's feet."

He didn't really mean that they needed to scrub each other's toes. But just like the example that Jesus set for them, they should be willing to serve each other in the same way. It's an example for all of us, to be so willing to serve others that we would even wash their feet.

Jesus, help me lead like You,
To go wherever You go;
Jesus, let me love them like You,
From their heads down to their toes.

## Night night, Jesus.

What is one way that you could serve others?

# Jesus Lives

[Jesus] has risen from death
as he said he would.

—MATTHEW 28:6

It had been the worst three days of their lives. Jesus' followers had seen their leader arrested and hung on a cross to die. Jesus was supposed to be the One, the Messiah, their Savior. But now He was gone. Dead. In a tomb.

*Or was He?* When the two Marys went to the tomb to see Jesus, they found an angel there instead.

"He is alive," the angel said. Alive. *Alive?* How could it be? They had all seen what happened. How could He now be alive?

But it was true. Jesus had risen, *just as He said He would.*

And with that, God's promise to the world came true. Jesus was the Savior, the Messiah who saved the world from its sins.

Jesus, Jesus, He's alive!
He fought both death and sin;
He hung our sins upon that cross
And rose to life again!

Night night, Jesus.

What else does
Jesus say He will do?

# Go Tell the World!

"So go and make followers of
all people in the world."

—MATTHEW 28:19

**B**efore Jesus went back to heaven, He told His
followers one last thing. "Go."

In all of His time on earth, Jesus was teaching us,
teaching His followers. He was showing us how to treat
people. He was showing us how to teach people. He was
showing us how to live our lives in a way that made

God proud and in a way that made other people want to know more about God.

And now that His time on earth was finished, He was passing that job on to us. "Go and make followers of all people in the world."

Now you know what to do. *Go.*

Jesus, lead on, show me how,
How You want me to go;
I want the world to follow You,
To know the Jesus that I know!

Night night, Jesus.

What is one thing that you can tell others about Jesus?

# Not Like the World

"My peace I give you. I do not give
it to you as the world does."

—John 14:27

**W**hat does *peace* mean to you?
Quiet? Calm? The sound of rain? A big bubble
bath? Crickets chirping? A warm, crackling fire?

When Jesus left the world, He left us His "peace." But it's a peace unlike the peace of the world. It doesn't really mean no wars or fighting. Or a quiet house. Or even a bubble bath.

It's a calm feeling deep inside. It's knowing that you're loved by the King of the world. It's knowing that no matter what happens—even when there's yelling or crashing or booming—Jesus is there. And He gives you His peace.

It is a peace better than any that the world may offer. And it is a peace that only Jesus can give.

Thank You for the gift of peace,
A peace only from You.
I know that whatever may come,
Your peace will see us through.

## Night night, Jesus.

What makes you feel peace deep inside?

# Love Like Jesus

"This is my command: Love each other as I have loved you."

—John 15:12

Do you remember how we talked about loving your neighbor like yourself? We understand how to do that, right? It can be kind of hard. But we can do it.

Well, when we start thinking that's easy, Jesus pushes us a little harder. He tells us to love other people like *He* loved us.

Now wait a minute, Jesus. You want us to spend our whole lives loving people? Even if they don't love us back? You want us to love people no matter what? And You want us to give our entire lives so that they can know You better and live with You forever?

"Love each other as I have loved you."

Oh. Okay then. Let's do it. Let's love each other like Jesus did. Because Jesus asked us to.

Jesus, this won't be easy;
Who can love like You do?
But I'll give it my best shot
Because You asked me to!

## Night night, Jesus.

How can you love like Jesus?

# Be Brave!

"In this world you will have trouble. But be brave! I have defeated the world!"

—John 16:33

So many scary things can come at us in this world. There are little things like dark, stormy nights and falling off your bike. There are big things like a sick family member or moving far away from your friends. But no matter what comes at us, Jesus is bigger.

"Be brave!" He told us. "I have defeated the world!"

We read stories about Jesus being a sweet, little baby or a kind, caring man. But He is also a fighter, a warrior, a winner—against everything bad and evil and scary. He has already won that fight. He has defeated the troubles of this world.

So be brave. And trust in the Winner, the One who has won the fight, the One who is on your side.

Thank You, thank You, Jesus,
I'll be brave and strong tonight;
Thank You, thank You, Jesus,
For already winning the fight!

## Night night, Jesus.

What troubles do you need Jesus to fight?

# Believe in the Lord

They said to him, "Believe in the Lord
Jesus and you will be saved—you
and all the people in your house."

—ACTS 16:31

After Jesus went back to heaven, His followers did exactly what He asked them to do. They got to work! They went out and started telling everyone about Jesus. They told people how Jesus had performed miracles, how He died and rose to life again on the third day, how He continued to eat with them and teach them even after He rose from the dead.

Then they would ask the people to believe, to believe and be saved.

It's that easy, you know. Just like John 3:16 tells us, whoever believes in Jesus will be saved. They'll have life forever with Him. And once we know Him ourselves, it's our job to tell others about Him, to tell them what we know, and to ask them to *believe* so that they, too, can be saved.

Jesus, please give me the words
To tell others about You;
Help me to help them understand
So they can be saved too!

# Night night, Jesus.

Who can you tell about Jesus?

# For the Good

We know that in everything God works
for the good of those who love him.

—Romans 8:28

Close your eyes for a minute. Picture God looking down on you right now. He's watching what you're doing, taking notes, moving some things around, making plans for your future.

Now, I don't know if He's actually taking notes

with a feather pen and a scroll of paper. But I do know this: He works for the good of those who love Him. In everything. Tiny things. Big things. Good things. Bad things. In all things.

That awesome thing you did? He took note. That sneaky thing you did yesterday? He saw it and will forgive you for it. Those people who were mean to you? He knows about them too. He loves you. He knows you. And He is working for your good.

Dear God, it's so good to know
You're looking out for me;
I know You're working to help me
Be the best *me* I can be!

## Night night, God.

How do you think God is working for your good right now?

# Pray Always

Pray at all times.

—Romans 12:12

**Y**ou know that you're supposed to pray when you have a problem. You may say a prayer before dinner. And you probably say a prayer at bedtime too, right?

But Romans 12:12 tells us that prayer is even more than that. Prayer is something that we can do at all times. When we're happy, when we're sad, when we're on our knees, or even on the playground.

God is with us everywhere, and we can talk to Him anytime at all! We can say, "Hey, thanks, God, for that beautiful sunset!" Or, "God, I really need to talk to You about something. . . ."

Prayers don't have to rhyme. They don't have to use big words. And they don't have to happen at the dinner table or by your bed. They can happen anywhere. Anytime. *At all times.*

God, thank You for being there
To talk to anytime.
I know You hear a lot of prayers;
Thank You for hearing *mine.*

## Night night, God.

What do you want to say to God right now?

# Love Is . . .

Love is patient and kind.

—I Corinthians 13:4

**Y**ou love your parents, right? You love your brother, sister, cousins, friends. You love your teacher, your neighbor, your grandparents, your great aunt. You love your dog. You love ice cream. (Okay, maybe ice cream isn't the best example.)

So what does love look like? The Bible tells us that, for starters, love is patient. And love is kind.

Are you patient with the people you love? Do you wait your turn? Do you wait patiently for dinner? Do you bang on the door when your big sister is in the bathroom?

Are you kind? Do you lend a helping hand? Do you call your grandma just to see how her day was? Do you give your pup extra scratches behind the ears for no reason at all?

All of these little things draw one great big picture of love. And love makes this world a bee-you-ti-ful place.

God, help me always to be
So patient and so kind;
Help me to care for others and
Keep their feelings in mind.

## Night night, God.

How did someone show you love today?

# Faith, Hope, and Love

These three things continue
forever: faith, hope and love.

—1 Corinthians 13:13

The Bible tells us that three things continue forever.

It's not popsicles or butterflies or tennis shoes. It's not dolls or blocks or swing sets. It's not ABCs or 123s.

The three things that last forever are faith, hope, and love.

So it would be smart to spend our days, our lives, every single moment on the things that really matter, on those things that last forever. Our faith. Our hope. Our love.

Get to know God. Believe in His promises. Love Him and His people.

In doing so, you will be using your life for things that truly will continue forever.

God, I want to live my life
For things that last forever;
With a little faith, hope, and love,
Life only gets better!

## Night night, God.

How can you focus on faith, hope, and love in your life?

# So Many Blessings

God can give you more blessings
than you need. Then you will always
have plenty of everything.

—2 Corinthians 9:8

Think back about your day. What did you complain about? Did you whine about anything? Maybe your food was mushy, or you didn't get to watch your favorite show, or you had to take a bath *again*.

But let's think for a minute. Do you have clean water to drink? Do you have lights in your home? Did you have food to eat today? Then, dearest little one, you have *plenty*.

Sometimes we get wrapped up in the things that are fun and the things that we like and the way *we* want things—which is totally okay sometimes. But we also need to remember that we have everything we need, *more* than everything. God gives us *plenty*.

God, look at all these blessings—
Look at what You do for me!
I couldn't count them if I tried;
Thank You, always, for plenty!

## Night night, God.

What do you have plenty of?

# When You Are Weak

"When you are weak, then my power is made perfect in you."

—2 Corinthians 12:9

**H**eroes are strong. Superheroes are stronger. And we're always trying to show everyone how big and strong we are.

There's nothing wrong with that, really. But it's also okay to be weak.

Actually, it's even better than okay. It's *perfect*. God says so.

When we are weak, when we feel like we can't do any more, when we ask God to come in and be our strength, His power is made perfect in us. He becomes our power in our weakness.

And when you think about it, is there anything stronger than that?

Thank You, God, for helping me
When I can do no more;
With You, when I'm at my weakest,
I'm even stronger than before!

## Night night, God.

How does God make
you feel strong?

# The Best Fruit

The fruit of the Spirit is love, joy,
peace, patience, kindness, goodness,
faithfulness, gentleness, self-control.

—GALATIANS 5:22-23 NASB

Have you ever watched an apple grow on a tree? It starts as a little flower blossom. Then the tree feeds it as it grows and grows from a tiny, sour, green ball into a big, juicy, red apple.

Did you know that the Spirit of God gives us fruit

too? Love and joy. Peace, patience, kindness. Goodness, faithfulness, gentleness. Self-control. We've talked about several of these together already.

They're all super-sweet fruits that are growing on the tree of *you*. And as you continue to spend time with God—talking to Him, learning about Him—these fruits will continue to grow in your heart and in your life.

Dear God, help me as I learn
To grow the sweetest fruits;
Kindness, gentleness, self-control—
They all point back to You.

## Night night, God.

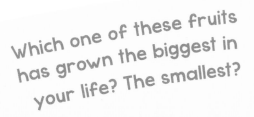

Which one of these fruits has grown the biggest in your life? The smallest?

# That Love

I pray that you can understand
how wide and how long and how
high and how deep that love is.

—EPHESIANS 3:18

This is my prayer for you, little ones.
As you grow and learn, learn and grow, you will
feel the love of Jesus in your life. It may come as a hug
from a teacher, wise words from a grandparent, or a
gentle breeze on a hot, summer day.

But you will feel it, and you will *know.*

Then, just when you think you know "how wide and
how long and how high and how deep that love is," He
will do something else. And you will realize
that His love is even bigger than you
ever thought it could be. Time and
time again, you will see His love.

And it will continue to grow—and amaze you with how much He loves you.

I pray that, now and forever, you can understand that love.

Jesus, I may never know
How far, how deep, how wide;
But I know Your love is there;
I feel it deep inside.

## Night night, Jesus.

How big is Jesus' love?
Can you describe it?

# Ask God

Do not worry about anything.
But pray and ask God for
everything you need.

—Philippians 4:6

**W**hat are you worried about? Anything? Something? Everything?

As humans, it's completely common for us to worry. But why? We have the God of all creation on our side. A mighty, powerful Father. And He is listening!

When you feel that little worry bug creeping in, don't listen to it. Don't sit and stare at it. Do exactly what this verse tells you to do.

Pray. "Pray and ask God for everything you need." Tell Him all about your worries, fears, and needs.

When you realize that God is in control, when you realize that Someone bigger and stronger is taking care of things, those little worry bugs scatter back into the darkness where they came from.

God, I know You're bigger than
All my worries and fears;
I know I can tell them all to You
And You will always hear.

## Night night, God.

What are you worried about right now? Give it to God.

# God's Peace

The peace that God gives is so great
that we cannot understand it.

—Philippians 4:7

There is a lot of crazy in this world. A lot of bad things happen. There are a lot of things we just don't understand.

And when this world feels too big, too scary, and too crazy, you can depend on God to give you peace. You may feel calm in the middle of a crazy day. You may smile when everything around you says to frown. You may laugh for no reason at all!

This all comes from a joy, a peace, deep inside of us. It was put there by our Creator. And it grows every time we talk to Him, turn to Him, depend on Him.

He will give you peace.

God, the peace that You give,
I cannot understand.
But I know I can depend on You
And hold tight to Your hand.

## Night night, God.

Imagine your hand, your life, being held by God.

# Think Good Thoughts

Think about the things that are
good and worthy of praise.

—Philippians 4:8

**W**hen you're mad or sad or worried, when your mind is busy and full, or even when you're upset and don't know why, think about what you're thinking about.

It sounds simple. But often we think about bad things all day long and then wonder why we feel bad. We wonder why we're antsy. We wonder why we're mad.

Thinking about what we're thinking about will help to bring us peace. When we turn our hearts and minds and eyes to things that are "good and worthy of praise," it makes us feel better.

When you're in the middle of something bad or even if you're not, make sure you look toward the good things. Find something good in every day, every moment, and it will make your heart happy.

Help me always to focus
On the good things around me.
You've given so many blessings;
Let them be all that I see.

## Night night, God.

Count all of your many blessings, and start right now.

# I Can!

I can do all things through Christ
because he gives me strength.

—Philippians 4:13

When you're feeling little, or when you're feeling weak, this is the verse that will bring you strength. There is great power in this verse if you believe it, if you know in your heart that it is true.

Memorize it. Write it down. Hang it on your mirror. Tell your friends.

Because you can, you know. You can do *all* things. When you're working with Jesus to do the things that Jesus wants you to do, He will give you the strength you need to make it through.

You're not too little, too small, or too weak. You have the power of an almighty God behind you. You can do anything. You can make it through anything. You can do *all* things in Jesus and through Jesus because He is the One who gives you strength.

Jesus, what would I ever do
Without You by my side?
With You, I can do everything!
I know this deep inside.

## Night night, Jesus.

Say it out loud: "I can do all things through Christ because he gives me strength."

# Always Give Thanks

Always be thankful.

—Colossians 3:15

O oh, this is a tough one. "Always be thankful."

*Always? Even when I'm in trouble?* Always.

*Even when it's rainy, and I can't play outside?* Always.

*Even when my big brother ate all the cookies?* Always.

We can always, always, always find something to be thankful for.

For a mom and dad who love us. *Always.*

For rain to water the flowers. *Always.*

For the smell of cookies and a brother to play with. *Always.*

Find that thing. And be thankful. *Always.*

Dear God, help me to see
The good in everything;
Help me to be thankful—*always*—
No matter what life may bring.

## Night night, God.

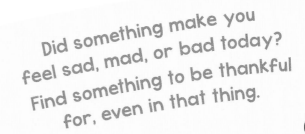

Did something make you feel sad, mad, or bad today? Find something to be thankful for, even in that thing.

# You Are Important!

You are young, but do not let anyone treat you as if you were not important.

—1 Timothy 4:12

**D**o you ever feel forgotten? Looked over? Not important?

Well, I'm here to tell you that it's not true. The Creator of the entire universe sees you and knows you.

He calls you by name. "God even knows how many hairs are on your head" (Matthew 10:30). You are a miracle from God, created by Him, created for a purpose.

If anyone ever treats you otherwise, like you're not important, like you have no purpose, like you're too little to matter, believe me, it's only because they can't see what God can see.

He can see the past and the future. He can see inside your heart. And He knows how wonderfully made you are—because He made you Himself!

You are important, made by God, known by God, and loved by God. Don't you ever forget it.

Dear God, I know I'm little,
But I'm also loved by You;
With You, I can do anything
That You want me to!

**Night night, God.**

What did you do that was important today?

# Be an Example

Be an example to show the believers
how they should live. Show them
with your words, with the way
you live, with your love, with your
faith, and with your pure life.

—1 Timothy 4:12

Because you are so important to God, the way you live matters.

Even when you're young, you can be an example for others. Someone younger than you can be looking up to you. Someone older than you can be looking down at you. And someone who doesn't know God may be looking over at you, just to see what that looks like.

For all of those reasons, show others with your actions how to live the right way. "Show them with . . . your love, with your faith, and with your pure life."

Someone is watching you. Be a good example for them.

God, help me always to be
An example of Your love—
For those watching all around me,
For You, watching from above.

## Night night, God.

What is one way that you can be a good example?

# Your Superpowers

God did not give us a spirit that
makes us afraid. He gave us a spirit
of power and love and self-control.

—2 Timothy 1:7

God gave us superpowers. Did you know that?
No, we can't fly. We don't have X-ray

vision. We can't make ourselves invisible. God gave us superpowers much stronger than those.

God has given us "a spirit of power and love and self-control." With those superpowers, we can stand strong when everything around us is falling. We can magically turn frowns into smiles. We can fight sadness with a single hug. We can defeat the evils of the world with the truth of God.

We may not look like the superheroes you see in the movies. But we are fighting a different kind of villain. And to do that, God has given us the superpowers that we need.

God, help me as I go out
And fight evil for You!
With power, love, and self-control,
Who knows what I can do?

## Night night, God.

What can you conquer with power, love, and self-control?

# It's Alive!

God's word is alive and working. . . .
And God's word judges the thoughts
and feelings in our hearts.

—HEBREWS 4:12

There's something really, really important that you need to know. This Bible that we keep talking about, it's not like any other book you've ever read before. It's not a fairy tale. It's not a tall tale. It is *absolutely not* a made-up story.

The Bible is from God Himself. It is "alive and working." It can tell us things about God. It can tell us things about ourselves. And it changes and grows, and we change and grow—even though the words stay the same.

You will read it today, and it will mean one thing to you. You will read it in a year, and it will mean something else. Don't ask me *how* it happens. I just know that it does.

Keep God's Word, His "alive and working" Word, with you. Get to know it well. It will change you, like no book ever before.

Thank You, God, for Your Word,
For the way it speaks to me;
It tells me all I need to know
To be the best I can be.

## Night night, God.

What is your favorite verse from the Bible?

# The Lord Cares for You

Give all your worries to [God],
because he cares for you.

—1 PETER 5:7

Wouldn't it be nice if you could give all your
worries away?

Oh, wait! You can! First Peter 5:7 reminds us that we

can pack up all of our worries into a big box and hand it over to God.

God cares about you. He really, truly does. And He doesn't want you to waste your time here on this earth worrying about everything. Matthew 6:27 tells us, "You cannot add any time to your life by worrying about it."

So why let your worries weigh you down? Give them to God.

He will take care of them, and He will take care of you.

God, here are all my worries;
I'm giving them to You.
I know that You'll take care of them,
And I'll feel better too!

# Night night, God.

Take all of your worries, wad them up, and toss them up to God.

# You Are God's Child

He loved us so much that we
are called children of God.

—1 John 3:1

Think about how much your parents love you. They
spend their days working and planning for you, to
give you everything you need and then some. They read

you stories at night. They snuggle you close. They dry your tears. There's no way you could imagine how much they love you.

Just like your parents, God loves you so much that He calls you His child. But unlike your parents, He is God. He can love you with an infinite love. He knows every single thing about you. And He loves you anyway.

He created you. He adores you. He calls you His child.

You, little one, are a child of God. Believe it. Know it. Live like it.

Dear God, it amazes me
That You call me Your own;
Your love for me is the greatest
That a child has ever known.

## Night night, God.

What is one way that God shows you He loves you?

# Go Away, Fear!

Where God's love is, there is no
fear, because God's perfect
love takes away fear.

—1 John 4:18

D on't be afraid." It's easy to say. But it's not so easy to
do, is it?

So why does the Bible say it over and over again? "Don't be afraid." "Fear not." "Be brave." Well, for one, it's because the Bible is full of God's love. And "God's perfect love takes away fear."

The Bible tells us that God loves you. He's watching over you. He's got good plans for you. He's working everything out for your good. And all of those promises leave no room for fear.

When you start to feel fear, remember God's love all throughout the Bible. Feel His love deep in your heart. And finally, tell that fear to scram!

Thank You for Your love that shouts,
"Get out of here, you fears!"
With a heart full of perfect love,
There's no room for that stuff here!

## Night night, God.

Close your eyes. Feel God's love filling up your heart and chasing all the fear away.

# The One Who Loves Us

[God] is the One who loves us.

—Revelation 1:5

Near the end of the Bible, in the very last book, we are reminded: "He is the One who loves us."

It's a good way to sum up the Bible, isn't it? Through it all, through the ups and downs, the fears and the doubts and the worries, the bad guys and the bad times, the heroes and the miracles, it's all about Him. It's all about God. God is there. And He is the One who loves us.

He is the One who is fighting for us. He is the One who takes our fear and doubts and worries. He is the One who gives us the power to fight the bad in the world, who helps us to be heroes, who lets us see miracles. It's all Him. It's all God.

And He is the One who loves us.

You are the One who loves me,
Even with my doubts and fears.
Through all of the good and the bad,
I know You'll be right here.

## Night night, God.

How does it feel to know that God loves you?

# Pictures of Heaven

The Lord God says, "I am the
Alpha and the Omega."

—Revelation 1:8

God tells us that He is the Alpha and the Omega. It means that He is the beginning and the end. God is the beginning and the end.

He is the beginning of the Bible and the end of the Bible. He is the beginning of your day and the end of your day. He is the beginning of the world and the end of the world. And He is there with you through it all.

He has been here since before the world began. He will be there when we're all together in eternity. And He will be there everywhere in between.

He was with you at the beginning of this book. And He will be with you long, long past the end.

Never stop looking for Him. Never stop learning about Him. He will never stop loving *you*.

The Alpha and Omega,
The beginning and the end—
God, when I think I've learned it all,
I'll start all over again.

## Night night, God.

What have you learned about God? What do you still need to know?

# About the Author

**A**my **Parker**'s children's books have sold more than a million copies, including two Christian Retailing's Best award-winning books and the bestselling books *A Night Night Prayer*; *Night Night, Farm*; *and Night Night, Train*.

## About the Illustrator

**Virginia Allyn** has illustrated more than a dozen children's books. She lives above a chocolate shop in a beautiful New Hampshire village. She enjoys collecting children's books, hiking, and eating all her vegetables (except peas).

# Also by
# Amy Parker

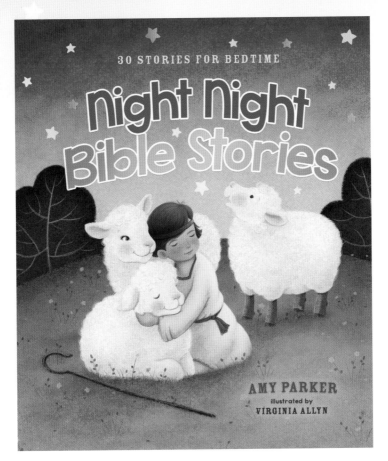

30 STORIES FOR BEDTIME

## Night Night
## Bible Stories

AMY PARKER

illustrated by
VIRGINIA ALLYN

Available wherever books are sold!

# Other Night Night books by
# Amy Parker

9780718088316

9780718089320

9781400310036

9780718090869

9780718042462

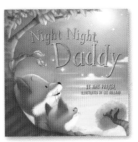

9780718042301

9781400318254

9781400324316